THE CHANGING FACES OF
Thame
BOOK THREE

Marilyn Yurdan

Series number 64

OTHER TITLES IN THE *CHANGING FACES* SERIES

	Series number		*Series number*
Abingdon: Book One	60	Grimsbury	31
Banbury: Book One	19	Headington: Book One	5
The Bartons	34	Headington: Book Two	8
Bicester: Book One	27	Headington: Book Three	62
Bicester: Book Two	37	Iffley	36
Bicester: Book Three	47	Jericho: Book One	13
Bicester: Book Four	51	Jericho: Book Two	39
Bicester: Book Five	58	Kennington: Book One	38
Blackbird Leys	48	Kennington: Book Two	53
Bladon with Church Hanborough and Long Hanborough	18	Kidlington: Book One	52
		Littlemore and Sandford	6
Botley and North Hinksey (Book One	3	Littlemore: Book Two	46
Botley and North Hinksey: Book Two	35	Marston: Book One	7
Chipping Norton: Book One	42	Marston: Book Two	12
St. Clements and East Oxford: Book One	14	North Oxford: Book One	23
St. Clements and East Oxford: Book Two	17	North Oxford: Book Two	30
Cowley: Book One	1	Oxford City Centre: Book One	29
Cowley: Book Two	4	Oxford Covered Market	63
Cowley: Book Three	41	Rose Hill	43
Cowley Works: Book One	25	South Oxford: Book One	24
Cowley Works: Book Two	54	South Oxford: Book Two	33
Cumnor and Appleton with Farmoor and Eaton	10	South Oxford: Book Three	56
		Thame: Book One	59
St Ebbes and St Thomas: Book One	15	Thame: Book Two	61
St Ebbes and St Thomas: Book Two	20	Thame: Book Three	64
Easington: Book One	45	Summertown and Cutteslowe	2
Eynsham: Book One	16	West Oxford	22
Eynsham: Book Two	26	Witney: Book One	28
Eynsham: Book Three	55	Witney: Book Two	44
Faringdon and surrounding villages: Book One	40	Wolvercote with Wytham and Godstow	12
Faringdon and surrounding villages: Book Two	49	Woodstock Book One	9
Faringdon and surrounding villages: Book Three	57	Woodstock: Book Two	21
Florence Park	50	Yarnton with Cassington and Begbroke	32

Published by
Robert Boyd Publications
260 Colwell Drive
Witney, Oxon OX28 5LW

First published 2008
Copyright © Marilyn Yurdan
and *Robert Boyd Publications*

ISBN: 978 1 899536 90 0

All rights reserved. No part of this book may be produced, stored in a retrieval system, or transmitted, in any form or by any means, electronic, mechanical, photo-copying, recording or otherwise, without the prior approval of the publisher. Marilyn Yurdan has asserted her right to be identified as the author of this work.

Printed and bound in Great Britain at the Alden Press, Witney OX29 0YG

Contents

Acknowledgements	4
Section One: Fun and Games	5
Section Two: More about Thame Pubs	29
Section Three: Schooldays	43
Section Four: Back to Businesses	57
Section Five: Amenities Past and Present	73

Cover illustrations

Front cover: The Spread Eagle Hotel.

Back cover: The dancing troupe at John Hampden Primary School, 1987.

Acknowledgements

Many thanks are due as always to Peter Forsyth, Julia Hussey, Shirley Phillips, Philip Shewry, Raymond Shewry, Peter Timms, *Newsquest Oxfordshire* and especially Janet Eaton, Chris McDowell and Peter Arnold.

Shortly before this book was published, we were saddened to hear of the death of Andy Arnold who has been a source of great help and encouragement in the writing of the Changing Faces of Thame books. Andy is pictured here in his youth.

Further Reading

J Howard Brown and W Guest, *A History of Thame*
A Hickman and D Bretherton, *Thame inns discovered*
N Pevsner and J Sherwood, *The Buildings of England, Oxfordshire*
Thame Town Guide 2007/8
Victoria County History, Oxfordshire, volume VII

www.lordwilliams.oxon.sch.uk
www.oldtamensians.co.uk
www.thame.net
www.thamehistory.net
www.thamemuseum.org
www.thameshow.co.uk

SECTION ONE

Fun and Games

Organized sport has a long history in Thame from the compulsory archery practice held in every parish after church on Sundays to the minor football teams whose faces peer proudly out of faded sepia photographs. Despite their impressive names, many clubs failed to survive but most modern sports are represented in the town today. Among them are cricket, tennis, table tennis, bowls, basketball, boxing, fencing, racquets, rugby, snooker, badminton, gymnastics, squash, running, martial arts and water sports. The Jubilee Swimming Pool funded by the Town Council and consisting of main pools and fun pool, a climbing castle, water slide, waterfalls and cannons and bubble loungers, was opened by the Countess of Wessex in 2003.

Apart from the Thame United ground in Windmill Road, football matches were traditionally played on the Rec in Southern Road but now there are facilities at Church Farm Recreation Ground. The old Rec has been joined by reation grounds with play areas at Elms Park in Park Street, the Churchill Play Area at Churchill Crescent, to the north-east, Pearce Way and Pickenfield to the south-east, Queen Elizabeth Circle off the North Eastern Distributor Road and the Skate Park at Church Farm.

Before the opening of the Sports Centre in the Oxford Road, Thame Sports Club was the mecca for serious players with the Bowls Club, founded in 1924, fronting onto Queens Road and tennis courts behind it. Playing tennis there could be something of an ordeal, for woe betide anyone who failed to take the game seriously although too high a standard in younger players would invite the attentions of the green-eyed monster as two or three of the elders were competitive to a fault.

Another set of tennis courts was to be found in the Orchard which was situated behind the gardens of the houses in Southern Road. One user remembers that he and his friends were made only too aware of the fact that they were second-class players, well below those who were members of the Sports Club.

Until the Wenman School opened, the very limited facilities which schools possessed were for the use of their pupils only, unlike today when most schools allow the public access at certain times. Now there are sports and fitness venues throughout the town.

One unusual venue was the War Memorial Club where there was a roller-skating rink, while snooker and billiards were played at the 'Stute' (presumably short for Institute) which was above the Fire Station in Nelson Street. Today there are premises for playing similar games at Thame Snooker Club in Wellington Street.

Sports Day at the Girls' Grammar School before its move to Holton.

Football has been called the Beautiful Game and in Thame there have been more football sides than any other sports teams. Among the past and present teams have been Thame United Football Club, Thame Reserves, Thame Minors, Thame Dynamos, Thame Corinthians, Thame Thursdays, Thame Saturdays, St Mary's (Thame) Football Club, Cross Keys Football Club, Thame, Boys, Youth and Girls Football Club and of course the various school teams.

A winning team from the 1908/9 season.

FUN AND GAMES   7

Bob Arnott's team, also taken during the 1908/9 season.

A Thame side which played against Chipping Norton in 1913.

The Thame Thursdays Football team in the mid-Thirties, back row: J Ing, G Fulkes, Reg Phillips, J Chowns, J Russell, - -. Front row: L Trafford, B Arnott, Ron Phillips, F Phillips, T Eele. They had just beaten Highfield Rovers 3-2 in the semi-final of the Thursday League but lost to St Frideswide's.

Thame United in the late 1940s: players include J Phillips, E Cadle, C Saunders, P Harbour and F Phillips. After difficulties which resulted in United having to leave the Windmill Road ground, and share one with Aylesbury United, in 2008 plans were announced for a move to a site adjacent to the Church Farm pitches on the ring road.

FUN AND GAMES 9

Thame Secondary School team 1947/8, back row: A Carpenter, J Quartly, R Shewry, G Chowns, G Broom, M Leigh, W Shirley, R Locke, middle row: P Spokes, N Summersbee, A Howlett, B West, T Crockford, R Eele, R Dix

Lord Williams's School soccer team in 1971, with fashionably long hair, but no perms!

On 1st April 1983 as part of a fun football contest held over the Easter school holidays, an all-girl team, the Seven Wonders, took part despite the disapproval of the Oxfordshire Football Association. Officials threatened to put an end to the Under-twelves six-a-side contest because a girls' team had entered. However, the organiser, Ray Boulton, defied them saying that it was nothing to do with the Association, being a series of 'friendly' matches involving about a hundred children. In the event the Seven Wonders lost all the three games they played against the boys but a mixed team captained by a girl did reach the semi-finals. These were the QPR Magpies from Oakley and the captain Laura McAllister of Seven Acres, Thame. The eventual winners were Chinnor Boys.

John Hampden Infants team in 1976.

FUN AND GAMES   11

The winning team from St Joseph's Roman Catholic School who beat Barley Hill in a junior six-a-side football tournament at the Sports Centre. From left, back: Matthew Ayres, Gareth Dunnaye, David Bitmead and Ross Mulligan, front row: Ben Pember, Sean Begley and Charles Bamford. Oxford United player Tony Obi was at the Centre where he offered help and advice to the young players in December 1986.

The Sports Centre under construction in 1981. The *Oxford Times,* writing on the lack of facilities in Thame on 5th June 1981, comments, 'The Southern Road recreation ground has pitches marked on it, and there is a shower room there. On Elms Park there are tennis courts, but that is the sum total of town council commitment to sports facilities for the town.' Oxfordshire County Council and South Oxfordshire District Council financed the major part of the Centre on the Lord Williams's School site in the Oxford Road.

The Sports and Arts Centre was officially opened by 90-year old Mrs Emma Sadler and five-year-old Richard Boulton, pictured here with Julia Brook in January 1982. The centre cost £370,000 and is open to all age groups not only from Thame but also the surrounding villages. Until it opened, swimmers had to go as far as Aylesbury, Bicester or even High Wycombe, while players of many other sports also had to go outside the town.

Also at the opening in January 1982, were the Thame Aces majorettes who gave a warm welcome to the new Centre.

FUN AND GAMES   13

John Maxwell and David Whetstone juggle and play the accordion to draw attention to the special mini-bus service to the new Centre.

Robert McCreery, coach at the Centre demonstrating a forehand drive at a coaching session in July 1983.

14   CHANGING FACES OF THAME

Letting off post-Christmas energy, youngsters bounce around on a giant inflatable in December 1987.

On Saturday mornings more than 100 youngsters gathered for the Junior Sports Club organised by Fred Bransby in May 1985. Aged between 4 and 13, members had their own club T-shirts and badges.

FUN AND GAMES 15

Reg Stevens from the Sports Centre gives expert archery tuition in July 1986 to Richard Boulton who, as a five-year-old, had been co-opener of the Centre.

SWIFT BADMINTON CLUB

SEASON OPENS

at
The Wenman School
Towersey Road, Thame
on
Monday, September 30th
at 6.30 p.m.

New members should contact the Secretary, D. A. Clewley, 23 Victoria Mead, Thame.

The Swifts Badminton Club advertisement for new members in the *Thame Gazette* in 1963.

The Oxfordshire Bowls side which played South Africa in 1953 included players from the Sports Club at Thame.

This cricket match played on the Rec between staff of the Town Hall and the Board of Guardians was captured by local photographer Harry Manistre at the turn of the 20th century. It seems to have been a 'friendly' as not all the players are wearing whites.

FUN AND GAMES 17

Lord Williams's School cricket field at about the same period.

Here is Lord Williams's (Lower East (School) cricket team which lost the Oxfordshire Schools' under-13 League Championship by one run on the Corpus Christi College sports ground in July 1983. Back row: Martin Rackham, Norrie Parmar (master in charge), Philip Plater, Middle row: Craig Surman, Tim Jordan, Michael Bateman, James Mitchell, Mark Priest (scorer and reserve), front: Barrie Edmonds (twelfth man), Grant Stoneman, Alan Maule, Michael Griffiths, Mark Busby and Lee Fortnam.

18   CHANGING FACES OF THAME

In November 1983 nearly 60 boys took part in BMX races at the Centre and 16 of them cycled from Aylesbury to be there.

Shown learning the basics of ice hockey in February 1984 with no ice and no skates, are from left: Nick Tribe, Nick Babbington, Matthew Ball, John Talbot, Sarah Thomas, Matthew Lord and Laura Lord.

FUN AND GAMES 19

**THAME
WAR MEMORIAL
:::
ROLLER RINK
RE-OPENS
WEDNESDAY
SEPTEMBER 22nd
at 7.30 p.m.**

An advertisement in the *Thame Gazette* for the War Memorial Roller Rink, 1954.

A conga on wheels in July 1986; roller skating at the Sports Centre during the school holidays.

This is Lord Williams's under-15 rugby squad pictured with the Robert Benoir Challenge Trophy which they won in Switzerland in May 1985. This was awarded for 'excellent discipline, sportsmanship, and entertaining open rugby' despite the fact that they did not win the tournament which took place at Nyon. Back row: Steven Davis, Barrie Edmonds, Ade King, Jason Gray, Martin Rackham, Elliott Wright, Paul Hudders, Tim Harper, Adam Hannam, front row: John Bartliff, Mark Priest, Tim Fairn, Grant Stoneman (captain), Jonathon Byrne, Julian Bailey, Daniel Horgan.

One event in the 11th Festival of Sport based at the Centre was the 10 km road race which was won in July 1986 by Paul Eales of Windsor, Slough and Eton Runners. The Race has become an annual affair which now takes place at the end of June.

Runners at the massed start at the beginning of Thame Festival of Sports in July 1984. This was the brain-child of former town and district councillor Derek Hurrell who identified the need for a sports and social club which workers at the firms on the industrial estate could use. Shops and businesses were interested in the project and so the Thame Industrial Sports and Social Club came into being.

Lord Williams's School Fitness Fun Run in October 1986.

In October 1981 Lord Williams's School team beat Wheatley Park by six points to win the Oxford Schools Sailing Association's first team competition at Farmoor reservoir. They fought off competition from ten other schools to carry off the Commodore's Cup. Team members were Maxwell Reid, Hugh Miller and Robert Kettle, Chris Wright, Richard Woods and Martin Groves.

In August 1984 one of the main attractions in the BIC pool was the inflatable octopus.

FUN AND GAMES 23

Dancing too has its fans, from the energetic Morris of Towersey Morris men to the more sedate Old Time Dances held in the Town Hall.

Towersey Morris Men performing outside the Swan in December 1982. Thame no longer has its own Morris side although there is mention of dancing in the churchwardens' accounts for the 16th century.

Petticoats Lost helping raise money for charity in March 1990; £140 went to Oxford Language Resource Base and £50 to Helen House Hospice in Oxford.

Advertisement in the *Thame Gazette* for a Sports Club Dance in 1946.

Advertisement in the *Thame Gazette* for the Folk Dance Club, 1947.

FUN AND GAMES 25

> **THAME AND DISTRICT M.C. AND L.C.C.**
> *present your*
> # MICHAELMAS DANCE
> at the
> ## SPREAD EAGLE HOTEL BALLROOM
> ### SATURDAY, OCTOBER 2nd
> Dancing 8 p.m. to midnight
>
> ERIC WAKEFIELD'S
> ## BARNSTORMERS
> under the direction of
> Victor Beaney
>
> Spot Prizes   Licensed Bar   Refreshments
> ADMISSION 5/-

A Michaelmas Dance advertised in the *Thame Gazette* in 1954.

> # OLD TIME DANCING
> EVERY WEDNESDAY
> Commencing October 2nd
> at the
> The Cygnet Room
> The Swan Hotel
> 8—10 p.m.
> Instructors Mr. & Mrs. B. Yarnold
> ADMISSION 2/-

> **THE NORA LANE SCHOOL OF DANCING**
> (Principal. Miss Nora Lane; Assistant: Miss Lucy Gordon) has re-opened for the Autumn Term.
> Tuesdays:
> At the Town Hall, Thame.
> Thursdays:
> At the Methodist Schoolroom, Thame
> Ladies' Physical Culture Class Thursdays (on and after Sept. 30) At the Methodist Schoolroom.
> Full particulars from 17 Langham Mansions, Earls Court Sq., London, S.W.5.

An advertisement for Old Time dancing (left) from the *Thame Gazette* in the 1960s. For those in need, plenty of tuition was available at the Norah Lane School of Dancing (right) based in London. Ladies could also attend Physical Culture classes which sound very different from today's aerobic sessions.

26 CHANGING FACES OF THAME

In July 1992 a treasure hunt was held at the Sports and Arts Centre as part of a programme of events organised by Lord Williams's School. The entrants are shown studying their questions before they start off.

Not everyone gets pleasure from taking part in physical activities for a mental workout can burn up the calories as well.

A Saturday morning Chess Club session at the Sports Centre in January 1983. Left to right Jeremy Storey (11), Keith Underwood (6), Timmy Storey (8) and their teacher, Ray Boulton.

FUN AND GAMES 27

Three members of Thame Chess Club, winners of special awards for progress and sportsmanship in April 1983, pose with their trophies. They are, left to right Robert Lagdon (9), Daryl Arnold (10) and Robert Jameson aged 11.

WORKERS' EDUCATIONAL ASSOCIATION.
Under the auspices of the W.E.A.
A COURSE OF TEN LECTURES on
THE HISTORY OF THAME
will be given by
W. GUEST, Esq., M.A. (Oxon)
In the Market Room, Spread Eagle Hotel
Beginning weekly from **Wednesday, October 4th, at 8 p.m**
Fee for the Course: 5/-
All who are interested are invited to attend.

Workers Education Association classes advertisement in 1950 for a series of lectures by W Guest, the writer of a classic history of the town.

28 CHANGING FACES OF THAME

> **FURTHER EDUCATION IN THAME & DISTRICT**
>
> ## WINTER PROGRAMME.
>
> COURSES and LECTURES in the following subjects:
>
> ART, BOOK-KEEPING, SHORTHAND, SINGING, DRESSMAKING, EMBROIDERY, COUNTRY DANCING, LEATHERWORK, PLASTICS, WOODWORK, HOUSEHOLD REPAIRS, Etc.
>
> LECTURE COURSES in HEALTH, HORTICULTURE, MUSICAL APPRECIATION, Etc.
>
> Enrol for these Courses at RYCOTEWOOD SCHOOL, 30, HIGH STREET, THAME, on Wednesday, Thursday or Friday, October 1st, 2nd and 3rd, from 7.30 to 8.30 p.m.
>
> Further particulars from The Secretary, Thame and District Advisory Committee for Further Education, Rycotewood School, 30, High St., Thame.

Night School, Winter Programme 1947. There was no shortage of subjects both practical and artistic for the people of Thame that year.

Pub games and quizzes are still very popular. This is Marathon Trivial Pursuit in progress at the Rising Sun in April 1991 when £1600 was raised towards buying a minibus for local autistic children.

SECTION TWO

More about Thame Pubs

Its pubs and inns are among the most prominent features of any English town and Thame has always been known for its fine examples. In the last half-century or so, however, they have been disappearing at a faster rate than at other periods and it may be of interest to note how many of those listed in the following poem called *The Inn-signs of Thame*, written by WR Church in 1867, have closed within living memory.

In every town we find the same
Queer names, like those we find in Thame.
More animals in Manders' cages
You'll hardly find than on these pages
We have a *Lion*[1] *Red* and roaring;
Also a *Cow*[2] p'raps *Red* from goaring;
We have a *Bull* just come from Wales[3]
A *Swan* which proudly by us sails.
The *Eagle* with majestic flight,
Towers proudly to the realms of light;
And then returns, without much fuss,
And stoops to draw the Railway Bus,
The *Fighting Cocks* have won the day,
The *Falcon* pounces on its prey,
The *Fox* is resting from the chase,
The *Greyhound* starts upon the race,
We have two Horses side by side,
A *White*[4] and *Black* just fit to ride,
The *Nag's Head* very fond of cricket,
Is always Batten !![5] at the wicket,
The *Saracen* has lost its head,
And he no longer can be fed;
The *Bell* is often made to ring,
With silvery tones by Mr King[6],
Four Horse Shoes point to roomy stables,
And steaming bowls and groaning tables,
The *Bird Cage*[7] once a dungeon dark,
Is now more fitted for a lark!
The Rifles here pile up their arms,
Nor care one rap for war's alarms;
The *Wool Pack* doesn't care a Rush[8]
Brittania's ready for a brush,
The *Half-Moon*[9] shines on rich preserves,

29

The *Anchor's* fast, it never swerves,
The *Old Blue Man* sticks up and grins
At the *Two Brewers* who are twins,
The *Six Bells*[10] ring Piercing tones,
The *Jolly Sailor* sits and groans,
The *Cross Keys* strive to stop the way,
And *Rising Sun* tells of the day,
And vainly strives to hide the light
Of those *Seven Stars* which shine so bright
On Lester's[11] head is placed the *Crown*,
The *Wenman Arms* have won renown;
The *Star and Garter*'s out of town,
The *Wheat Sheaf*'s heavy head hangs down,
The *Abingdon* and *Oxford Arms*
Are opened wide with many charms;
The *Plough and Arrow* bravely toil,
To rob the ground of golden spoil,
Thus ends my list, thus ends my rhyme,
P'raps some will say yes, 'tis quite time.

NOTES: [1] Red Lion. [2] Red Cow. [3] Wales, name of landlord. [4] White Horse, Black Horse. [5] Batten, the name of landlord. [6] King, the name of landlord. [7] Bird Cage, headquarters of Rifle Corps. [8] Rush, the name of landlord. [9] Half-Moon, frequented by poachers. [10] Pearce, the name of landlord. [11] Lester, the name of landlord.

Of the 33 establishments mentioned in the poem only 13 are still functioning, one of them, the Spread Eagle having expanded its name and another, the Oxford Arms, having altered it, first to the Market Place, then to Jimmy Figg's and afterwards an Italian restaurant called Prezzo. Some of these (the Britannia, the Half-Moon, the Woolpack, the Red Lion), have disappeared virtually without trace, some former pubs, like the Fighting Cocks (currently Woolworths), the Wheatsheaf (Cancer Research Fund), and the Seven Stars (Thame Tandoori), still have the brackets above them where the sign once hung while the Anchor's frame still has a Witch Ball and the Saracen's Head sign remains intact. Yet others, the Crown, the Plough, the Blue Man, the Four Horseshoes, the Greyhound, the Wenman Arms, the White Horse, the One Bell, the Fox, the Bull and the Jolly Sailor, have been converted into private houses or business premises.

As children in the 50s, we loved to go round into the courtyard off the High Street, just past the Post Office, to watch Stan Court at work in his studio. Sometimes when we got there he'd be painting the names of rowing men on college oars after Eights Week, but much more interesting were the pub signs. He'd start off doing a small version, about a foot square, and I remember he gave me one, the Blackbird, to take home. I kept it for years. There were the usual ones, the Fox and the Plough of course, but sometimes more uncommon ones from further away from places we'd never heard of, not just in and around Thame.

THAME PUBS 31

Stan Court and G Mackenney at work in the studio in 1955. As an article in the *Oxford Times* reported in February 1958, Stan Court designed and painted some 2000 in signs throughout fifteen counties, including all those in the Midlands.

The following is a selection of Thame pubs which did not survive into the new millennium.

In February 1980 regulars at the Fox managed to raise almost £100 in small change to help mentally handicapped children. Here landlady Mavis Flynn and Heather Goodwin break open a gallon whisky bottle containing £92.50.

The exterior of the Four Horseshoes when it functioned as the Railway Hotel.

As customers' tastes became more and more sophisticated, pubs needed to change with the times. It was no longer enough to advertise good stabling, garage space or even "Hot and Cold Running Water in all Rooms". Coming back from their package tours on the Continent and beyond, the people of Thame began to appreciate a much more varied cuisine and pubs started to compete in offering a wide range of dishes. Meals, and not just snacks, were served in the bar and some pubs went as far as opening their own restaurants on the premises. However, even this was not always enough to save them from closure.

The Four Horseshoes once included a ground-breaking restaurant called Whittaker's. Pictured are Stephanie and Peter Whittaker with catering and restaurant manager Kenton Locke in August 1994.

When we were growing up in the late Fifties and early Sixties pubs were very different from how they are now. For a start they didn't generally serve meals, all you could get to eat was a packet of crisps or peanuts or in the more go-ahead ones, pork pies or pasties. I can still smell the wafts of stale beer coming from the cool, dark interiors as you went past. There was very little going on inside, maybe a game of darts or dominoes or a friendly argument about rival football teams, certainly nothing violent. People would sit all night with a pint or two and if anyone had a drop too much they were funny rather than quarrelsome. I can't remember any would-be drinkers being questioned about their age. On Sundays we'd walk home via the Bird Cage where they sold ice creams from a little side door. We always had crème de menthe choc ices, the only time I've ever come across that flavour. The Abingdon Arms had an off-licence where we could take back empty bottles and get a penny or two on each.

The Abingdon Arms in April 1992 when the off-licence had become a separate shop.

The exterior of the Jolly Sailor in July 1982.

Jack Smith (right) and John Good pictured in the bar of the Jolly Sailor in December 1982. That year's Christmas decorations included at least 2500 miniature lights. One year they put up 4000 lights and another time about 40 Christmas trees. Television personality Larry Grayson was a frequent visitor. In 1985 the pub became the Wellington Hotel with accommodation for 35 guests but closed altogether in 1994.

THAME PUBS 35

December 1958 at the Saracen's Head where landlord J J Harrison and Mrs Harrison watch as George Bowler aged 73, a thatcher from Towersey, adds the 7500th penny to a stack collected for Thame Evergreen Club.

The exterior of the former Saracen's Head today, now Reaston Brown estate agents, but still displaying the signboard for the pub which closed in 1963.

Three generations of tenancy of the Fighting Cocks came to an end in June 1967 when the Howlett family had to give up the licence after 124 years. The demand for business premises in this prime location became so great that the Aylesbury Brewery Company Ltd sold the building which was merged with the one next to it in order to create an electrical showroom.

The start of the annual Thame Lions Club Pram Prix in November 1987. Twenty-two teams took part with 16 pubs to be visited en route where only one team member had to drink at each stop. The Race easily made its £1000 target to buy and train a guide dog for a blind person. The winning team, finishing in less than 28 minutes and receiving the Leyland DAF trophy, came from the Fox. In second place came the Star and Garter, with the Falcon A team third. The team from the Rising Sun A scored a double by winning the awards for both the best-dressed pram and for the most sponsorship with £221 collected.

Other pub and hotels are still very much a going concern and keep up with the times. In this picture taken in 1986 the Swan is closed while a new development complete with homes, shops and business premises is being constructed leading from the High Street through to Wellington Street. Outbuildings at the back of the pub were swept away. After searching for what the developers called a 'suitable name', they came up with Swan Walk.

Owners David and Sue Turnbull, with Gary and Sally Pielow and Maggie Peck in the restaurant of the Swan in March 1988.

In August 1985 builder Ted Bell from Towersey devised a computer program for use in the bar of the Black Horse when dealing with orders for meals. Landlord Peter Snow enters an order watched by Mr Bell.

This view of Cornmarket shows the old Spread Eagle sign still coming out of the wall instead of hanging from its frame, and facing it the Birdcage is without its storybook timbers.

Mrs Pat Ellis, landlady of the Birdcage pictured during an interview about the 12 years which she spent in the haunted pub and her acquaintance with Ghosty Boy, as she calls the supposed haunter. The *Oxford Times* had previously run a feature on the haunting in an interview with Mr and Mr Ellis at Christmas 1971.

Even after a change of licensee Ghosty Boy was still in residence in February 1994. Landlady Wendy Wade is shown on the old staircase leading to the haunted cellar at the Birdcage.

The restaurant at the Spread Eagle has always been known for offering good food. Chef Michael Thomas, Restaurant Manageress Samantha Edwards, with Sarah and David Barrington in December 1992.

In this picture taken in the 1930s, the Cross Keys is shown standing at the junction of equally deserted East Street and Park Street.

Far more interesting than the pubs themselves were the rooms which they hired out for parties. *In 1962 the Black Horse had a separate hall off Rooks Lane, the Four Horse Shoes had a hall round the back and the Cross Keys had an upstairs function room. They also provided drinks, and alcoholic ones at that, and glasses. All we had to do was supply some very basic things to eat and of course invite the guests!*

It didn't seem strange at the time that the pub landlords sold gallons of beer and cider to schoolchildren but, looking back, I suppose that one of our fathers must have taken care of the booking and other arrangements of that kind.

Here is a pub garden with a difference. . . it's indoors! Manager Michael Davy (right) suns himself with regulars Mick Frith, Mark Lampit, Kevin Morgan, Henry Eaton, Kim Servat and Julie Braham at Jimmy Figg's (now an Italian restaurant called Prezzo) in a previous existence in July 1990 when it was still the Oxford Arms.

The changes of name involved with this establishment are very unusual for Thame where pub names have remained the same for many years, sometimes for centuries. This is true to the extent that former pubs, now turned into private residences keep some mention of their former use as at the Old Plough, the Old Crown, Red Cow Barn and the Old Blue Man. The name the Oxford Arms is a long-standing one as is shown by the poem of 1867. Although unimaginative it is not controversial in the way that the King's Head was before it was felt prudent to change it to the Nag's Head after the beheading of Charles I, and it was not until the second half of the 20th century that this series of changes took place.

The Six Bells shown in about 1890. The bells in the pub's title are those of Thame Abbey. The sign later read first Inn in' and 'Last Inn out' which it was after the Crown had closed. The cottage nearest the pub is now part of it. The frontage today is mock-Tudor. *When we were about 14 or 15 we'd sometimes go into the Six Bells and be served our halves of lager and lime along with everyone else, and we were schoolgirls!*

Dave and Joan Simpson, licensees of the Six Bells in February 1994.

SECTION THREE

Schooldays

Although schooldays aren't necessarily the best days of our lives, they're among the most frequently photographed and pictures taken of the various schools in Thame date back over a century.

The Church of England Mixed School in Southern Road was often referred to as the Bottom School and later became Thame Secondary Modern School whereas the Top School is the John Hampden in Park Street, which celebrated its 170th anniversary in 2007.

In the late Twenties says Peter Forsyth, *there were 'red letter' days such as Empire Day, celebrated with due ceremony by gathering in the playground to march past and salute the flag, as arranged by the headmaster. It should be remembered that the First World War had only ceased eight years before this time and must still have been fresh in many people's minds.*

The Cookery class of 1922/3, from top to bottom, left to right includes: F Higgs, D Alcott, J Wagerfield, M Howse, - -, M Chowns, N Betts, C Eele, E West, H Richardson, D Harbour, D Howland, K Chowns, Miss Fowler, H Eaton, M Gilbert, - -, I Guntripp.

In this photo taken in 1908 at the Bottom School, note on the far right the man (or are there 2 men?) in Highland dress, attire not frequently seen in an Oxfordshire school.

A music class in c 1947/8 at what had by then become the Secondary Modern: at piano S Kinch, back row: M Hall, M Harris, H Baldwin, N White, in front: E Tew and B(?)Tew.

SCHOOLDAYS 45

Hampden House at the Secondary Modern 1947/8: including P Tew, P Wise, J Cole, B West, N Summersbee, B Cole, I Locke, J Rice, Brenda (Sheila?) Newitt, Mrs Fulford, M Harris, S Kinch, S Bambrook, V Baker.

This picture taken in the early 1950s shows the Secondary School garden complete with urn, pond and seat. The site is now part of Mitchell Close. The willow tree was included in the garden of the house called 'Hog Fair'.

Headmaster Frank Mitchell poses with pupils Vivien Walker, and Arthur Howlett who became a well-known footballer. Mitchell Close was named after Mr Mitchell.

Form 4 Girls in 1958: Top to bottom, left to right: J McKenzie, M Gomm, C Aldridge, S Wallace, A King, M Walters, R Graney, D Purnell, P Shrimpton, G Evans, M North, E Moran, G Harrison, J Romero, P Smith, P Burke, J Howlett, W Drury, D Bowler.

Form 4 Boys in 1958: top to bottom, left to right: R Chowns, D Bambrook, R Howse, R Kinch, C White, N Boiling, R Boiling, J Smith, A Adams, D Eldridge, P Adams, P Young, R Hurst, M Salter, F Davidson, S Baker, L Johnstone

At the top of the town was the Royal British School which opened in 1837, became the National School and finally the John Hampden. Peter Forsyth recalls how in the Twenties *the John Hampden itself instituted various initiatives (this is not a modern phenomenon), one was to 'clean your teeth' time promoted by no less a person than a gentleman from Gibbs Dentifrice. We were each given complimentary pats of dentifrice and then awarded a star, on a daily basis, on providing evidence (verbal) of cleaning, but the practice didn't last very long. The idea was good, children's teeth at that time were particularly bad and although school visits by the local dentist happened, there was an inbuilt fear of that gentleman, usually well founded.*

In addition to the two primary state schools within the town, the parents of Thame children had the option of sending them to the private school run by Miss Margaret Woods in Queen's Road or further afield to St Theresa's Convent at Princes Risborough. Children from Thame and the surrounding villages like Long Crendon, Tiddington, Towersey and Kingsey, were taken by coach to and from the Convent and the fact that very few of them were Roman Catholics is proof of its good reputation.

Pupils from John Hampden Infants admiring Lollipop the guinea pig who managed to survive a cold October night after making a bid for freedom in 1977. On the left is Andrew Spokes who, with his mother Christine, found Lollipop on their way to school.

The retirement of schoolteacher June Cray in July 1981 after 16 years at the John Hampden Infants' School was marked by a day out in the grounds of Waddesdon Manor

SCHOOLDAYS   49

Fruit and vegetables, including beetroot, carrots, marrow and bananas, which were brought to the John Hampden in Oct 1981 for Harvest Festival, were divided up and given to three local causes. Pictured with some of the produce are Andrew Gillard, Lisa Campo, Melanie Allum, Simon Howarth and Elizabeth Turnbull.

In June 1981 Pat Slater (centre) got up at 3 am to go to Billingsgate to buy fish for her stall at a fete at the John Hampden Junior School. She's shown with helpers James Burley and Peter Waycott.

There are two other junior school schools in Thame in addition to the John Hampden. Peter Lewis and Nicholas Brant, pupils at Barley Hill School, are shown planting trees in March 1983. They had raised £25 to buy two trees, a wild cherry and a double weeping cherry, by selling toys and making cakes.

In October 1986 parents and children prepare to clear the overgrown garden of the John Hampden Primary School. It had been disused for about 5 years but was turned into a wildlife area to be used for environmental studies. The site also included a restored greenhouse and a pond

A Wendy Shop built by Gordon Daly, appeared at St Joseph's School in June 1991. With the builder are Jack Stevens, Lucy Brown, Katherine Gaughan, David Birthill, Thomas Atkinson and Sarah Moss.

52   CHANGING FACES OF THAME

In August 1960 a new secondary school, the Wenman School, was opened.

Prizewinners at the Wenman School in July 1970, front left: John Drury, Josephine Johnson, David Perry, Colin Belgrove, Deborah Johnson and Alison Slater.

Mr RF More giving a geography lesson to pupils at Lord Williams's in July 1958.

In October 1982, an Indian week at Lord Williams's school included curry for lunch, Indian music over the tannoy and a demonstration of Indian dance. The pupils were shown how to cook authentic Indian food by Mrs Rakhamat Begum and Mrs Iqbal Fatima at Lower School West and the results of their cooking went on sale in the school shop. The picture shows Mrs Rakhamat Begum giving a demonstration.

In October 1982 sixty staff and students from Lord Williams's set off for Boston, Massachusetts, to spend a month on an arts tour including a performance of the musical 'Oh What a Lovely War!'.

Pictured in January 1984 are Andrew Gallagher, Andrew Hood, Matthew Wells, Lucy Blyth, Tom Baldwin, Peter Clarke and Susie West, six-formers from Lord Williams's who were all set to take up places at Oxbridge colleges.

In November 1984 after working for a term with poets John Loveday and John Cotton, forty poetry students at Lord Williams's School combined their work to produce a book which went into print. The scheme was sponsored by WH Smith and the Poetry Society and the booklet printed by the school's art department. Zoe Basford is shown reading her poetry to other young writers.

At Lord Williams's Schools Prize Day in July 1986 nearly £2000, raised by various sponsored events, was presented to three charities. Shown here are the Lower School West prize winners, from left: L Halstead, M Ball, V Heley, J Turner, I Thorogood, R Chaney and N Wall.

Janie Lea, Andrea Kilbridge and Suzanne Thompson, pupils at Lord Williams's School, obviously enjoyed interviewing 85-year-old Margaret Wood in November 1988 while collecting material on the oral history of Thame at Meadowcroft Home.

Teacher Malcolm Davies with pupils from Lord Williams's Lower School and some of the items which they put into a time capsule in June 1994. From the left: M Rantle, J Hazeldene, N Hill, S Johnson, R Christu, A Denham, D Allen and J Unsworth.

SECTION FOUR

Back to Businesses

Traditional sales pitches: a view of the Tuesday Market in November 1980

Shops in Middle Row around the beginning of the 20th century. The one on the right, Number One Cornmarket, is the tobacconist and confectioners belonging to the Misses Walker.

Like most lads of my age [in the Thirties] *I had to do a good deal of the shopping. We had our milk delivered to the door by George Oliver with his pony and rap with a churn on board, ladling the milk from a highly polished bucket, which he carried to the door, into proffered jugs etc. but for pretty well all else it was down to the shops with a basket and shopping list. My mother was critical of some of the produce that I used to bring back reckoning that I had been fobbed off with poor quality, particularly with regard to meat! I always feared the embarrassment of having to take things back.*

As regards the groceries etc I was on firmer ground with other shopkeepers, it was he butchers that were the problem; my aunt worked in the International Stores, so I liked to patronised that establishment, but we had Miss Limmings next door and Mr Briers across the road so we were spoilt for choice. Fruit and veg was another problem area, my father was no gardener, and in any case we had no room for growing vegetables at the back of 89 Park Street, but I was always happy to shop at Mrs Fleet's. And on the shops in Park Street, *then followed Peggy Lemmings's small grocery shop and further down, with large glass windows, was Will Horton, plumbers and sanitary ware, with Tillie Horton and poor 'Candle' Horton wandering around. On to Jackman's, bakers, confectionery and post office, Child's antiques, to Philip (Pincher) Wells groceries. It was generally believed that the nickname Pincher arose from the fact that on one occasion when he was serving a customer with plums he had pinched one in half to obtain the correct weight!*

Newman's Stores was built on the site of the former rifle range in Park Street. Between 1931 and 1973 it was known as Hunt and Reading's or Rhoden's Stores.

I remember as a very small child [in the Twenties] *going to a pantomime, Bluebeard, presented in some premises behind Hunt and Reading's grocers shop.*

BACK TO BUSINESS

Raymond Shewry's *Old Thame of the Past* is bound to bring back quite a few memories!

'Oh for the Thame I used to know,
All those many years ago,
Miss Lester with her china shop,
Sergeant Lord, our local cop.
Redman and **Bukely** were the drapers,
Castle's and **Holland's** for toys and papers.
Chemists **Barley** and **Brand** for medicines and pills,
Doctors **Rowlands, Beer** and **Stevens** tended our ills.

In order to equip a bungalow or house
You could buy furniture from **RJ Rouse**.
Misses Plumridge and **Saunders** for chocolate and sweets,
Mrs Shrimpton and **Percy Bingham** just down the street.
There were **Harry Rose, Austin's** and **Hawkin's** for suits.
Copes and **Freeman, Hardy and Willis** for shoes and boots.
Up in the High Street more shops could be found,
Mellet's for leather - the best around.
There were **Price, Howes** and **Purcell, Jones** and **Fleet,**
Wright's, Cohen and **Stevens** - he too sold meat.

Martin and Silver for wool, cloth and silk.
Quartly's, Blunt and **Jim Holland** delivered the milk.
Bishop's for fish, both fried and wet,
Major Kidd who was the vet.
The Gas Works with its grey, gigantic tanks,
Barclays, Lloyds and Westminster were the banks.
Fred Edden with threshing drum driven by steam,
Mr Viner kept our windows bright and clean.

Top of the town, more shops galore.
Leming's, Hunt and Reading, Fulke's General Store.
Willoughby's, Limming's and **Rhoden's, Jackman's** for bread,
Messrs Tarry and Humphris to bury the dead.
Ralph Timms, Fred Bowler, blacksmiths by trade,
Mr Soames, famed for hurdles and gates that he made.
Coalmen, **Howland and Bush, Bambrook's** and **Wright,**
Eatons made wagons - a wonderful sight!
Tanyard, Auto Dairies, Pursers - names of the past.
Pearce the wool staplers - one who did last.
Thame Mill Laundry, another who has moved on.
Potters Agricultural Machinery, they've also gone.
Gone too, the pickle factory with its tangy smell.
Bus depot, railway station, they've gone as well.
Now we have big new industrial sites,
Where factories produce goods both day and night.

Jackman's Cafe - a local meeting place,
Percy Dobson for fruit and fresh plaice.
Ironmongers **Potters**, and **Mr Lewis**
Whose hands were worn,
Bakers **Styles, Huntleys** and S**awyers,** and Hughes for corn.
Cycles could be bought from **Betts, Hasler** and **West,**
And our local Thame butchers were the best.
Jordan's, Baileys, Elton, squires - to name a few.
Shrimptons and **Bartons** to paint things for you.
Ashdown's for dresses, **Walker's** for seed,
Quainton and **Arnott,** good cobblers indeed.

Hester's and **Grimshaw** for jewellery and clocks,
Howland's, Holland's and **Bonner** for bricks and blocks.
Holland's Electrical, **Bird's** and **Reg Bailey'**
The **Co-op** and **International** to serve our needs daily.
To keep us smart and debonair,
Deverell, Airlie and **Loader** to groom our hair.
Midwife **Nurse Gubbins** in whom many put their trust.
Local Councillor and dentist, **Basil Rust.**
Care of the eyes for perfect sight,
Tranter was there to put things right.

Garages **Price, Brazell's, Service Station** and Baker's,
West also supplied cars for the undertakers.
Thame Haulage whose lorries travelled near and far,
Haseler's and **Bambrook's** for the hire of a car.
Thame's local dance band, **Frank Payne's Red Aces**
Tassy Johnson for paraffin, sweets and bootlaces.
Admired by all from dawn to night,
Flowers at **Walker's** nurseries - a lovely sight.
Headmasters **Mitchell** and **West** of schools in the town.
Jim Arnold organised Thame Show of famous renown.
Mr Seymour supplied market stalls, served milk out of a can,
Mr Jones and **Reg Newitt** - the railway station they ran.
In those days we had the '**Grand**',
We even had our own town band.
Dances were held most Saturday nights,
Very rarely were there fights.
All this 'progress' has been made
To try to built a 'better' Thame.
Has it all been worthwhile I ask,
Or money down the drain?

Anyone needing to travel between the top and the bottom ends of the town was likely to go by bike or, if they were really up-to-the-minute, by car. This picture of Parker's Engineer and Cycle Agent, perfectly illustrates the transitional stage between cycling and motoring.

The south side of Cornmarket and High Street in October 1961 showing long gone businesses, some of them mentioned in the above poem: the Gents' Hairdressing Salon, the Fireside Sweet Shop, Huntley's bakers and snack bar, the Fighting Cocks, Lightfoot and Lowndes, solicitors, Potters ironmongers, Rose's tailors and the former Girls' Grammar School.

Some premises continue to use their former names long after the businesses they refer to have closed. The Witch Ball was on the site of the former Anchor public house. In this picture dated 18th December 1964 Mr and Mrs T Evelyn Swain pose with a witch ball from which their antique shop took its name. Now estate agents Simmons and Laurence occupy the premises but the Witch Ball's sign remains to this day.

Ford's Electrical, taken in 1968, gave a taste of the shops of the future. Housed in part of the converted Fighting Cocks premises, its stock consisted of items that would have previously been seen as luxury goods but were increasingly to be found in most homes of the period.

This evocative picture, taken in February 1981, shows Wright's Bakery. *In 1962, when I was in the Fifth Form, I used to have a Saturday job in the Wool Shop and was sent along to Wright's to get the owner's bread. The shop smelled wonderful with the whiff of fresh baking that you don't get with today's wrapped bread. The names of the loaves were new to me, split tins and bloomers and milk loaves. Occasionally she'd ask me to bring cream horns, or éclairs or meringues as well.*

In November 1981 the local press ran a feature on shopping in Thame. Here Audrey Moon displays some of the merchandise which she and her sister Joan Whalley sold in Moon's of Thame at 3 Upper High Street.

Also from November 1981, Ann Davis in the confectionary and tobacco shop in the Buttermarket which she ran with her husband Michael.

Older Tamensians will certainly remember Annie Saunders whose shop this used to be. It sold sweets and tobacco for more than a century. Thame was always well supplied with shops selling sweets, chocolate and ice cream Apart from this one and the one at No 1 Cornmarket, there was the Fireside Sweetshop opposite the Town Hall, Goshawks (previously Plumridge's), on the corner of Pump Lane and Cornmarket and Mrs Price who sold all sorts of things like sherbet fountains, and gob-stoppers, flying saucers, Black Jacks and fruit salads, usually 4 for a penny, from her home in Upper High Street.

Number 4 Upper High Street featuring Mrs Price's sweet shop.

Peter Arnold, remembering the early 50s, writes: *from the left it shows part of No. 2, where Aubrey and Pam Blunt (Aubrey managed Potters for many years) lived, Mrs Price's sweetshop (with Mum and Dad's bedroom, part of No. 4, above it), and No. 4 itself, with the large half-door and my bedroom above it, and Granny Downie's room above our sitting room. Wow! I can smell it all now! Mrs Price was immensely special to me. I must be one of the few children who were provided with dummy cigarette packets to play with. The large Players and Wills advertising packets, which first spent time in her shop window, before being passed to me, were very well made and withstood a lot of childish handling! The smell of tobacco! (And, from slightly further up the street, the smell of leather, from Brackenbury's... and of coffee, from Jones's Café... and of meat, from Jordan's... and of 'pub inside', from the Swan...) Heavens! I AM getting old and sentimental!* Number 4 has recently been opened up and now houses the Helen and Douglas House charity shop.

November 1981 Taurus china and glassware shop in Buttermarket, once Bullingdon House where Frank Mundy had his wine vaults, is now Essence. The vine growing up and across the front of the shop yielded 29lb of grapes the previous year. Manager Jean Martin who used to tend it, said the grapes were rather sour to eat but excellent for making jelly.

In March 1984 Dave Carthew was celebrating South Oxfordshire District Council's decision to allow him to extend his business by converting the adjoining cottage into a fish-and-chip restaurant. This move was controversial but it was decided that Thame needed a small cheap place to eat in the area. The chippie was formerly Kimberley's and is now the Dragon Inn.

It was strange how you'd always feel hungry when you went past Kimberley's even if you'd just had your tea. Probably the smell of the vinegar. We used to get fish and chips in newspaper and take them down Moorend Lane. They were always hot enough to burn your fingers when you pulled the fish apart. When we'd finish we'd stuff the paper into the hedgerows so it wouldn't blow about. It wasn't built up down there like it is today and there were no litter bins.

In December 1983 traders in Upper High Street protested against road-works which threatened to damage their Christmas trade due to the parking spaces being out of use. They hired a van which they parked outside the Birdcage. All over the side of the van were notices telling shoppers not to be put off by the road-works. John Butler and Rosemary Spencer are shown at work in the temporary shop.

BACK TO BUSINESS 67

The original Pied Pedaller when it was a cycle shop in the High Street. It later transferred to the site of the Grand Cinema in North Street.

Philip Goodall shown at the Pied Pedaller in October 1991 after it had become a toy shop. The shop closed in 2008.

February 1988 David, Delia and Herbert Smith pose outside their shop on the corner of North Street. The shop's sign which read 'H & D Smith Sons and Daughters', was supposed to be a novelty.

However, this earlier picture shows that the naming was not original as it was used by 'Jockey' Leigh and family in the 1950s and 60s. Before this it was Lesters and is now Zen Hair Design.

The first shop to let you pick out your own produce was Walker's, the Lashlake Nurseries people, where you could take a basket and walk round to choose you own fruit and veg and take it to the counter to be weighed and priced. They also had a frozen food cabinet. One day, it must have been in the mid-Fifties, Mum and her friend went in there and fancied getting something different for tea. They came home with frozen chocolate éclairs which looked absolutely yummy. We were so disappointed when we found that we'd have to wait for them to defrost and we'd expected to eat them straight away, like ice cream.

The stocking of frozen foods was quite innovative at this time on the part of Walker's as by no means everybody owned a fridge, let alone a freezer. In Thame at least, the frozen ranges, initially only Birdseye, took a long time to become popular as using frozen food involved forward planning in that time had to be allowed for it to defrost but could of course not be bought in advance and just put away in the store-cupboard and used whenever needed.

March 1991 Mrs Linda Honey, winner of a trolley dash competition at Thame Co-operative, flanked by Lions members John Busby (left) and Keith Lane

Shops in the Lower High Street in March 1985, currently (from left to right) Gallery Wood Flooring and Carpets and Mia Capri.

A sign of the times in April 1989. Manager Reg Salter is shown outside Austin's menswear shop where vandalism forced the management to put up new steel shutters.

These stretched across the little arcade between Austin's two display windows before Greyhound Walk was constructed to give access to Waitrose and on into Greyhound Lane. The open arcade was used as a meeting place for young people, the small minority of whom had done a considerable amount of damage including painting graffiti, making holes, breaking a padlock and forcing their way into the garden at the rear of the shop. As the shop is in a conservation area, the Town Council didn't like the appearanceof the shutters, but agreed that they were necessary.

Winners of the Book House colouring competition in August 1985 received books as prizes. Shown here with books and winning entries are Amy Enticknap and Leanne Sherwin.

Towards the end of the 20th century a new type of shop appeared in the country's High Streets and Thame was no exception. Just as second-hand clothes shops and jumble sales were becoming a thing of the past, the charity shop appeared and mushroomed.

January 1995 The opening of the Shaw Trust charity shop in Lower High Street by Colin Deveraux who played Doris the Cook in that season's pantomime at the Swan Theatre, Wycombe. With him is shop manager Liz Wilkins.

November 1995: workers at the Cancer Research Fund relax with a glass of Beaujolais nouveau. Shown left to right are Selwyn Petterson, Polly Bossom and John Ethell.

SECTION FIVE

Amenities Past and Present

Sir Robert Peel's first police force was set up in London in 1829 and proved such a success that ten years later local authorities were given the power to set up similar forces which were answerable to the Justices of the Peace of the county in Quarter Sessions. This became compulsory in 1856.

Thame County Police Station was built in 1854 and was one of the first in Oxfordshire. Before it opened, prisoners were either taken off to Oxford prison or else the constable kept them in his own home where he had to sit up all night with them.

Before the construction of the County Court House in 1861, courts had been held in the assembly rooms at the Spread Eagle. The Coroner's examination which decided that the Thame Hoard was Treasure Trove was held in the Spread as late as May 1940. The Petty Sessions took place in the old Market Hall, forerunner of the present Town Hall. The Court House itself was closed in 2003 and converted into a museum of Thame history.

The Old Police Station which was situated between the Chinnor and Thame Park Roads. The present one is in Greyhound Lane.

Thame's first fire engine was bought by public subscription. About 1817 the sum of £158 11s 6d was raised by 134 contributors and in 1818 an engine was bought for £79 17s. Hose, buckets and other essential equipment was also bought. In 1841 a public meeting was called in order to discuss the problems caused by the shortcomings of this engine and seven years later things came to a head when it was found to be faulty at the scene of a fire.

In 1878 a fire brigade was formed under HH Smith and three years later its members won the main prize at a competition in Aylesbury. A new fire-engine station was built opposite the Whitehound pond in Upper High Street where it later became No 23. The Ordnance Survey map of 1888 shows a Fire Engine House in Park Street, opposite the brickworks. For years the pond was the main water supply until in 1880 a drain was constructed underground connecting the pond to a tank at the corner of High Street and North Street although this was not completely successful.

At the beginning of the 20th century the fire crew would get be paid for their services by insurance companies and the money would be shared out when they returned from the fire. There was an annual outing to the seaside by train with the brigade having its own coach on the Great Western Railway.

Fire Engines outside the old Fire Engine House, probably in 1878.

AMENITIES PAST AND PRESENT 75

A group of prize-winning firemen posing in the earl Sixties.

Peter Arnold remembers: Grandfather Arnold, was a fireman; my Dad, when young, used to have the job of running down from 26 Nelson Street to Windmill Road, to bring the fire engine horse to the Fire Station, when there was a "shout". I can certainly remember being awoken by the furious ringing of the night alarm bell on our landing at Upper High Street, and seeing Dad running across Upper High Street: he was among other things, a retained fireman. When we used to have big family teas at Grandmother's in Nelson Street, we could always tell if the fire engine was about to be called out: the siren took so much electricity to start up that all the house lights dipped. We would then be given permission to run down the road and watch the firemen arrive: the Bambrooks coasting to a halt in one of the family's taxis; Rupert Timms pedalling furiously up the street and throwing his bike into the Fire Station hedge; Chris Wainwright running straight across Upper High Street from the Swan... If I'd stayed in Thame I'd have been a retained fireman!

A fire-brigade 'shout' at an office building in the High Street in October 1996.

After many years in Nelson Street, the Fire Station is set to move.

An ambulance station built in Southern Road, near the corner of Spring Path lay derelict for many years until its site was built on in 2007. The drivers, of whom one of the most notable was Bill Pearman, were not paramedics as they are today.

The town's Post Offices have occupied various sites with a central one and smaller branches in Queens Road and Park Street. In the early days post offices were little more than places where stamps were sold in unperforated sheets but as they gradually offered an increasing range of services, larger premises were needed.

The Thame office started off in Grimsley's shop in the Butter Market then moved to what was later the site of Barclay's Bank. Premises later occupied by the Co-operative stores followed, then Mears' printing works. HT Mears acted as postmaster from 1861 to 1890. During his time came the move to the ground floor of 91 High Street where it remained until 1903 with more space for sorting. A move to No 101 (The Shrubbery) came in 1903.

Peter Abethell, who came out from Oxford to work at the Post Office on relief towards the end of the Sixties, recalls *When anybody mentions Thame I always remember the time that I was staying in a pub nearly opposite the Post Office. I could see it from my window. One morning, when I'd been given the keys to open up, my clock had stopped during the night. When I went to the window, opened it and stuck my head out to see what the Town Hall clock said, I noticed a queue already waiting for me outside the Post Office. I've never got dressed so fast before or since!*

AMENITIES PAST AND PRESENT 77

Early wall-mounted collection boxes arrived in East Street and Priest End in 1877 and were important enough to be marked on the 1888 Ordnance Survey map.

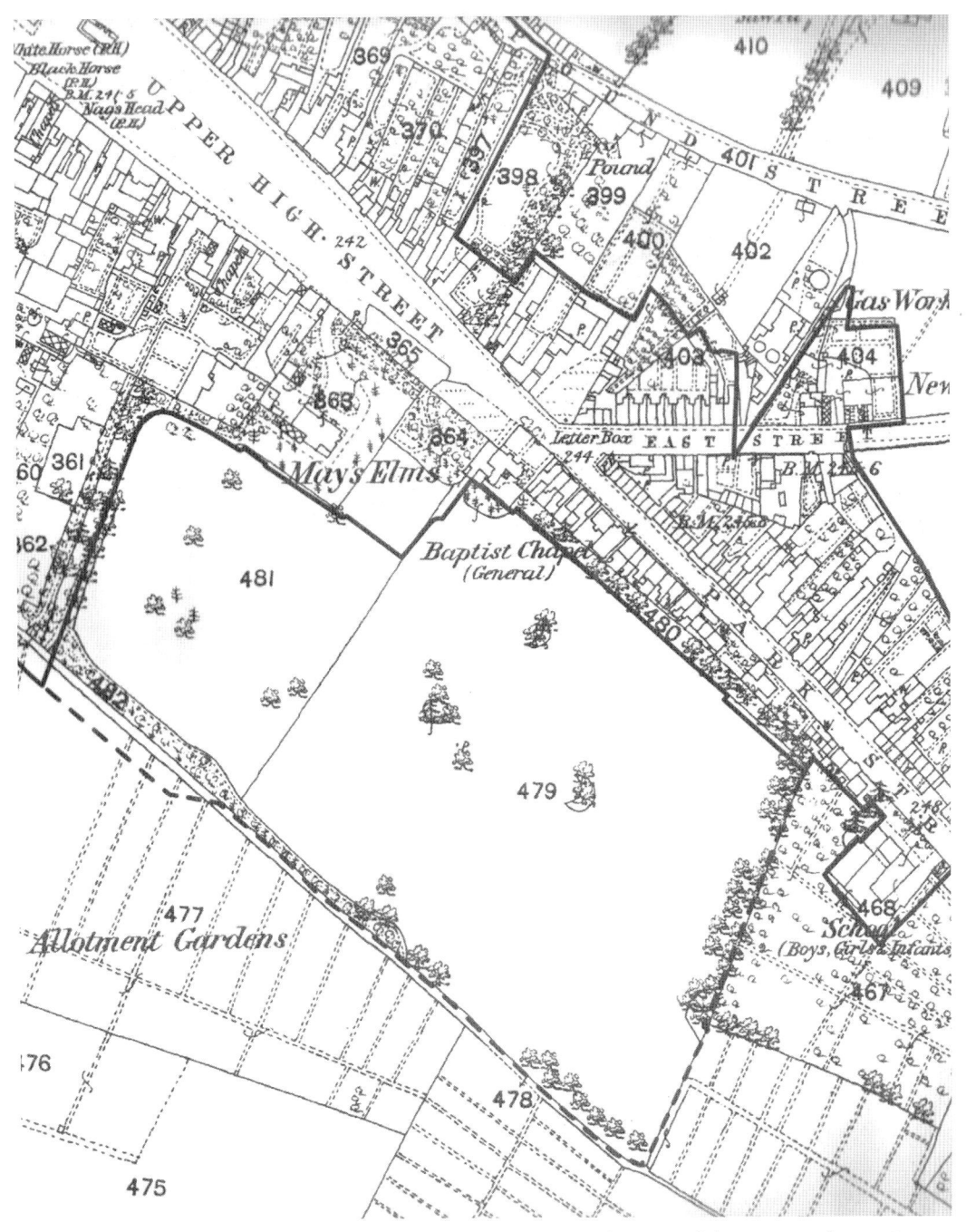

Ordnance Survey map 1888 showing post at the junction of Upper High Street and East Street.

Postcard of a delivery cart and postman outside the premises at 91 High Street.

One family involved in delivery the mail from the 18th century onward were the Websters whose ancestress Fanny Bickerstaff was responsible for distributing the post to addresses between Thame and Brill. This meant a walk of up to 35 miles a day, 20 being frequent. She was escorted by her husband, a peddler. The letters were wrapped up in a handkerchief or carried in a basket and Mrs Bickerstaff would have been welcomed with refreshments by those lucky enough to receive mail. On one never-to-be forgotten occasion a letter was seized by a pet monkey while the post lady was busily chattering at the door.

Fanny died in 1838 at the age of 62. Michael Webster, one of her sons, was 42 years in the postal service and in 1840 was the first person in Thame to carry the newly introduced penny post For this he was paid 8/- a week and wore a uniform of a top hat with gold band round it, paid for by the townspeople. He retired in 1878 but his sons John and Lawrence kept up the family tradition with 37 and 41 years of service respectively. Lawrence had to put up with the freak snowstorm of 18th and 19th January 1881 when the snow was neck-high in some places. By 1935 'Young Jack' Webster had put in 37 years service of his own.

In *Lark Rise to Candleford* Flora Thompson relates how, towards the end of the 19th century, her character Laura had to tramp round the countryside for miles in very much the same way that Fanny had done. There were letter-thieves lying in wait for Laura as well, in her case not a monkey but the footmen at the Big House who pounced upon her post-bag and used it as a ball.

AMENITIES PAST AND PRESENT 79

The former Post Office in High Street before the counter business was moved across to Martin the Newsagent. The sorting office is still in its old position at the rear of this building.

December 1990, Mrs Norma Laver (left) and Mrs Jenny Walker (right) from A Piece of Cake with a Thank You present for Martin Paul, Mrs Pam Kucel, Paul Fuller and Mrs Beryl Ponting, workers at Thame Post Office.

A Literary Institute was founded in 1845 to further 'general knowledge, to check intemperance and immorality, and to rouse to higher and worthier objects.' Lectures suitable to this purpose were offered, as well as popular reading, recitations and concerts in the Market Hall. Members would drop in to the Institute to read daily and weekly newspapers and to borrow books from its library of some 600 titles although this facility was not well used. Unfortunately its members could not always be relied on to behave as well as the organisers hoped. There is mention of their being caught playing cards for money and smoking in the games room, for the Institute gradually turned into a social club with about 60 members. Always in financial difficulties, it moved into smaller premises by taking two rooms in the Town Hall in 1888. When this was found to be inconvenient to the Town Council, it moved again to the former post office at 91 High Street and membership increased. This led to games, billiards and a reading room and even a resident caretaker.

This postcard includes a view of the Literary Institute at 91 High Street.

The former library in Upper High Street is shown before its move to Southern Road. The library will at some point move into the old Grand Cinema site in North Street now that the Pied Pedaller has closed.

The Grand Cinema shortly after it closed in 1967.

After its closure a committee was formed with a view to buying the building and reopening it as an arts centre. The idea was that it should be used by drama groups and let out for films, lectures, bingo and concerts. The purchase price of the cinema was £9,500 with a further £2,500 necessary to renovate and heat it. In the event it was turned into a toyshop, the Pied Pedaller. The first cinema in Thame stood on the corner of Croft Road and Chinnor Road.

This account of the Grand, written by Philip Shewry, will bring back lots of memories. *The Grand Cinema, scruffy, smelly and generally unlovely, was nevertheless the focal point for entertainment in the Forties and Fifties for the inhabitants of Thame. Throughout the War and before television became all-powerful, the cinema brought real pleasure to a great many people. An escape from everyday life.*

The Grand's appeal was universal although where you could afford to sit was some proof of your status, but not always; the back row downstairs was high on the priority list for amorous couples. However, the balcony was the most expensive and its occupants no doubt felt superior as they observed the masses below them.

The films changed twice a week and were mainly black and white, technicolor ones were that bit special. The Grand never opened on Sundays, its private owners being strict chapel. The format was generally the same: a "B" type Western, Hop-along Cassidy or Roy Rogers, the Gaumont British News, and then the main feature. During the War the films were heavy on propaganda and children's games were clearly influenced by what they saw on the screen. Adverts came along later and the local ones were often greeted with much derision.

Patrons of the Grand could be put into three main categories. The first were those that always went on Mondays and Thursdays, they just had to be there at the first showing as if this carried some sort of prestige. And it did in a way for they were able to pass judgement the following day, either at work or at school, as to the merits of what they had just seen and sometimes to reveal the story line gleefully. Some buffs of course just had to see the film at the earliest opportunity.

The second group were mainly the housewives, groups of friends who regularly occupied the same seats every Tuesday and Friday. During the War many of their husbands were in the Forces and of those who weren't many men preferred other attractions, not the least being the multitude of public houses in Thame. Children often went with their parents although on Saturday afternoons they had their own special programmes. Children wishing to "A" Certificate films had to be accompanied by an adult and to overcome this problem, some hurried liaisons were formed in the waiting queues.

The third group were the villagers who were bussed into Thame every Wednesday and Saturday evenings, quite an event in those days. A night at the Grand, followed by fish and chips eaten in transit, was the height of their expectations. Romances flourished and very often film-watching became secondary as the lights went down.

The Grand possessed no dishy usherettes; their alternatives were an elderly couple who lived next door and the male of the species conducted his business in the most autocratic manner. Known simply as 'Flint', he strode the aisles with a vengeance, his torch seeking out any sources of trouble. This usually constituted youthful exuberance and the culprits soon found themselves on the pavement outside. To be thrown out by Flint was quite an accolade but once was usually enough. And the Flints certainly didn't serve ice cream. When that became available it had to be purchased at the ticket kiosk, either when going in or at the interval. On very warm evenings it was just possible to nip over to the Wheatsheaf opposite for a shandy and still get back in time for the main feature, the Flints permitting of course. Flint was also very patriotic and woe betide anyone who tried to leave by the side doors before the National Anthem had finished.

The Grand had an aroma all of its own, a sort of ancient mustiness. It seemed to increase the nearer to the screen one sat. It didn't boast an organ pre-film entertainment was usually in the form of scratchy Victor Sylvester gramophone record. But nobody cared it was all about atmosphere, anticipation and excitement.

Opening time was seven p.m. and the next half an hour was to be savoured. Get the best seat, see who was there and who with. Look at the programme and relish the forthcoming attractions. Observe the Flints limbering up for the evening, torches at the ready. There were four prices for tickets. Balcony seats were dearest, they were 2/3d. About half a dozen rows downstairs cost 2 shillings; these included of course the much- prized ones at the very back. The bulk of the downstairs cost 1/6d and the cheapest seats, those at the front, cost 9d. The Saturday afternoon price for children was 7d.

The Grand almost certainly reached its peak towards the end of the War when the public's appetite was insatiable. The queues often stretched back into the Buttermarket and it was not unusual for many to be turned away.

There was one attempt one attempt to 'tart up' the Grand as the locals put it, but it failed miserably. It struggled into the Sixties and its new owners tried a few gimmicks including Sunday opening but its essential character was gone and it became quite a seedy dive and yobbish behaviour flourished with the fearsome Flints no longer a deterrent. It finally closed in 1967 – going to the pictures in Thame was over. If "video killed the radio star" television certainly killed the Grand.

The former Gazette Office building in the Shambles before the paper's move to Swan Walk.

The first issue of the *Thame Gazette* appeared on 11th March 1856. Costing 1d, it consisted of only 4 pages of which only one column contained local news, the rest being national and international news, market reports, and even politics. The price increased not long afterwards to 1½d and in 1862 the number of pages doubled and the price dropped to 1d.

The first Editor was Charles Ellis who held the post for nineteen years. In the 1880s appeared the *Thame Observer*, a liberal and non-conformist Saturday publication and on Thursdays the *South Oxfordshire News* under editor CH Jones. In 1890 the *News* was forced to pay out £25 in libel damages to Herbert Dodwell for alleged comments which it claimed that he had made during an election campaign. Although still very much alive, the *Thame Gazette* is no longer privately owned, being part of the *Bucks Herald* and *Bucks Advertiser* group.

As Ray Shewry mentions in his poem, the three original banks in Thame were the Westminster (NatWest) in the same position, Barclays, which was on the corner of Cornmarket where Coral Bookmakers is now, and Lloyds which is now Lloyds TSB. The present HSBC site was a garage.

When I joined the Westminster Bank in 1963 there was no computerization just an assortment of adding machines and one for doing the customers' statements. Even the calculations for the ledgers were by mental arithmetic and the entries written by hand. The balances were then called back and if there were more than three mistakes on a statement it was torn down and had to be copied out correctly. All the cheques and credit slips were sent out with the statements and the post taken down to the Post Office in the High Street in a brown cardboard case. As juniors we had to do this and bring back the empty case before we were allowed to go home in the evening.

One day, shortly before Christmas, Pete Timms and I were on post duty. Unbeknown to our superiors, Pete had in his possession a bottle of cherry brandy for his mother and he'd been sipping at it on and off all afternoon. As usual, we went the 100 yards or so to the Post Office on his scooter with me on the back, clutching the locked case. Pete jumped off the scooter, unlocked the case and shoved all the post into the mail box outside. When he came to restart the scooter, he look puzzled and then very sheepish. It turned out that he'd posted the scooter keys along with the bank's mail, so we had to go back inside, queue up again, and get someone to come and unlock the mail box from the inside and get the keys. After that, whenever we were on post duty we left the scooter at the bank and walked there.

In December 1976, an empty safe stands outside the National Westminster Bank in Cornmarket waiting to be collected and scrapped as part of an improvement programme which also included a new and ultra-secure safe.

In the 1960s customer relations were much more personal than they are now, mainly because people had to come into the branch to conduct their business in person rather than use the Internet or a cash dispenser. All the bank staff knew those who had plenty of investments as well as those who had lots swank but were always going overdrawn. At Christmas the staff could look forward to all sorts of offerings, ranging from home-made mince pies to tins of sweets and biscuits, bottles of wine and spirits and even a brace of pheasants (still in feather) for the Manager.

AMENITIES PAST AND PRESENT

A Tourist Information Centre opened in 1995 in the old Market House. The picture shows John East, Chairman of the Southern Tourist Board, flanked by Derek Lester (left) and Dr John Whitehead of the John Hampden Society, at the official opening ceremony. The Centre has been closed since 1st April 2006 in what first appeared to be an April Fool's Day joke. The Citizens' Advice Bureau and public toilets are still housed in the building. The toilets entered from outside the north eastern side of the Town Hall, never one of the main attractions of the town, have since closed.

For years the town's open rubbish tip, usually referred to as the Dump, was in Moreton Lane, between the Rec and the railway line, where Combe Hill Crescent was later built.

The dustmen used to come round every week and collect the bins. You didn't have to put them out yourself, they came up the garden path and round the back of the house. They were heavy too, made of metal, not polythene. The contents were tipped into the dustcart which had sections with covers that could be pushed up and down, a bit like on a breadbin. It was drawn by an enormous shire horse- I think his name really was Dobbin - which wore blinkers and stopped patiently every few yards. Sometimes one of the dustmen would lift us kids up onto the horse's back, miles from the ground, amongst all the jangling harness, and give us a ride for a few yards. Imagine that for Health and Safety! The tip was quite near us and we could sometimes smell it in hot weather when the wind was in the wrong direction, but it wasn't anywhere near as bad then, mainly paper, broken household things and vegetable peelings. Some people used to cycle up to the Dump and sort through the refuse. They had a trailer of the back of one of the bikes so it must have seemed worth their while I suppose.

A more up-to-date dust-cart eventually replaced Dobbin and his breadbin, and this one was motorized with an open section at the rear. So slow was its progress through the town that children would toss in apple cores. A regular and memorable sight was Annie Saunders, who kept a sweetshop and tobacconist in the Buttermarket, running along behind the cart, shaking her duster into the container at the back.

When the tip was moved from Moreton Lane, work soon started on the houses which were to become Coombe Hill Crescent and Conduit Hill Rise, so much better addresses than The Dump. There was none of the fears of pollution and poisoned earth that we hear about nowadays and the Dump had never been a source of annoyance. However, for the residents of a number of streets to the north of the town, a nightmare was about to begin.

The tip moved to Moor End Lane where its smells, smoke and flies became a nuisance to the residents of the new Lea Park estate, the Lashlake and Mill estates and Queen's Close. Lea Park residents organized a protest march to the Town Hall where they handed in a 200-signature petition. One of the most obnoxious tippings was the contents of the stomachs of slaughtered beasts by the Fatstock Marketing Corporation and the spraying of the contents of cesspit emptiers onto the tip. Local MP Michael Heseltine came to inspect the tip for himself.

A protest march heading for the Town Hall in June 1974.

AMENITIES PAST AND PRESENT

The bus garage in Bell Lane seen in 1968. There was never a bus station in Thame as such, the bus stances being as now outside and opposite the Town Hall.

Peter Forsyth found that in the Forties, *the Oxford bus service was good and reliable, although the buses tended to get quite crowded in the war years and getting a seat at Gloucester Green in Oxford for the return journey needed the use of the elbows (who said the British always formed orderly queues), but a relief bus always came along. The main grumble by Thame people was that theses buses got filled up by many who were only travelling as far as Headington.*

A town bus service operated by Motts Coaches was launched with high hopes in July 1985 but was forced to closed after only 3 years due to a shortage of passengers. Members of the Town Council were disappointed but not surprised as townspeople had been warned on several occasions that the bus would be discontinued if it wasn't used enough and was therefore uneconomical. It was subsidized by both the own Council and Oxfordshire County Council and made several changed to its route including visiting Long Crendon and Towersey, in order to attract customers.

A market-day service to and from Moreton followed and there is now a service which runs between the town centre and Cotmore Gardens.

Town Councillors at the launch of the bus service in July 1985.

Prior to the start of the town bus service there had been a shoppers' service to and from Towersey but that was all. In general people had to walk or go by bicycle if they wanted to get to places at any distance from the town centre. Pupils at Lord Williams's and Holton Park Grammar Schools had to cycle in from, say Towersey, and, in the case of the girls, leave their bikes and catch the school bus from the Town Hall to Wheatley. Not a pleasant prospect on dark mornings or evenings.

The residents of Moreton were always considered very courageous by any privileged town-dwellers who watched them set off into the darkness for their trek home along unlit country paths after an evening at the cinema, bingo or the fair. They would walk along in a group, chatting quite happily and presumably they were so used to their journey that they didn't give it a second thought.

An earlier transport casualty was Thame railway station, closed in 1964, and superseded by the Thame and Haddenham Parkway two miles out of the town on the Birmingham to London Chiltern Line. *The train service was, like all GWR lines at that time* [the Forties], *unreliable with regard to timekeeping and the inconvenient position of the station with respect to most of the population meant that it wasn't much used in the Oxford direction, but was needed for a reasonably fast trip to London via Princes Risborough, although some people preferred to take the bus to Aylesbury and change to a Green Line bus for London.*

AMENITIES PAST AND PRESENT   89

The engine-driver, fireman, and station officials looking suitably regretful on the occasion of the leaving of the last passenger train from Thame station.

The railway station pictured in June 1962, not long before its closure and already looking rather forlorn.

A dashing Jim Arnold, complete with cap and cigarette, posing in a carriage window of the last train.

This cheerful group includes historian Dr WO Hassall and Mrs A G Hassell, of Wheatley, who clearly took great pains with their appearance for this event though it is unclear why Dr Hassall chose to wear full academic dress.

AMENITIES PAST AND PRESENT 91

A horse trough, reminiscent of an earlier form of transport, used to stand in Upper High Street near the Elms, outside the enclosing wall of the Pearce memorial garden. With the disappearance of horse-drawn traffic it became redundant but was removed for safekeeping.

One amenity which fortunately has become unnecessary was the air raid shelter in front of the Town Hall. There was another shelter in car park in the Upper High Street on the roof of which a band played to celebrate the end of the War.

One of the parts of Thame which has changed more than any other is Moreton Lane, once an old-fashioned country lane leading only to the Rec and the Dump and bordered by tall hedges for much of its length. It is now a proper made-up road as far as Arnold Way and gives access to one of Thame's more recent amenities, which has been created almost literally from the ashes of a former one. This is the aptly named Phoenix Trail, a path which runs for seven miles and has been constructed along the lines of the disused railway. It forms part of Route 57 of the National Cycle Network built by the civil engineering company, Sustrans.

The Phoenix Trail is all on the level and therefore ideal for walkers, cyclists, horse riders and users of wheelchairs and buggies. It has already won a European Commission Certificate of Distinction and been designated a European Greenway. It is provided with plenty of seats and sculptures made by students of the former Rycotewood College.

Although the Trail at present only goes to Princes Risborough to the east, it is envisaged that it may be extended westwards as far as Oxford.

This aerial photograph taken in May 1964 shows several of the town's prominent features including the gasometer. Fred Lomas was one of the main men in charge of the Gas Works. Coke, a by-product, was readily available and widely used in Thame. The site of the gasometer, which gave its name to Gas Alley leading from East Street into Wellington Street, is now occupied by an Indian restaurant.

The water tower, once a feature of the skyline of the allotments nearly opposite the railway station has also vanished.

Thame's latest amenity seems set to become very successful. This is Thame Museum, sited at 79 Lower High Street in the former court building. It is run by the Thame Museum Trust, supported by Thame Historical Society and staffed by volunteers. One of its earliest exhibits is a series of late-16th-century wall paintings which were found initially in the 1930s at 34 Upper High Street. They were later rediscovered in the late 1960s and donated to the Oxfordshire County Museum which has loaned them to Thame Museum where they are housed in a reconstruction of their original site.

In the main showroom information panels include topics such as John Hampden and Lord Williams, and there are displays of old maps, local businesses and wartime Thame, Many items have been donated by Thame residents, past and present. A poignant memento of a local hero is the framed lock of John Hampden's hair which was removed from his coffin by William Smith when it was opened in 1828 to find out what he'd died of but the results were indecisive.

In the Community Room videos of old photographs are shown and there is a Resource Room. Thame Museum stages temporary exhibitions and acts as a focus for the findings of research groups such as the Thame Buildings Index and the compilation of various projects, records, guides and memoirs.

This mid-brown wedding dress is thought to have been worn by Caroline Betts when she married Tom Mott at the Primitive Methodist chapel at Moreton in 1875. The couple lived in Moreton where they brought up 12 children. Accompanying the dress is a photograph of Caroline taken in 1925 wearing it at her Golden Wedding party.

Museum members Janet Eaton and Shirley Phillips using the facilities of the Research Room.

In Cabinet 3 of the Main Gallery stands a replica of a musketeer from 'Colonel John Hampden's Regiment of Foote', complete with his accessories. He wears a woollen doublet in the regimental colours of green with a yellow lining, and a knee-length linen shirt which could be used as nightwear. He carries a 62" matchlock breech-loaded musket and his oyster hilt sword is in a scabbard hung from a baldrick. His accessories include a bandolier and bottles, a powder horn and a crucifix and he is surrounded by more items from his kit.

AMENITIES PAST AND PRESENT 95

A cotton night-shirt which belonged to the Edden family. The story of how, in 1828, William Noble Edden was murdered and how his ghost appeared to his widow to let her know his fate and accuse his killer, is well known locally.

The alleged murder weapon
Various hammers were produced at the trial of Solomon Sewell and Benjamin Tyler for the murder of William 'Noble' Edden on 5 March 1830. This is said to be a head from one of those hammers.

These buttons are said to be from Noble's coat.

Items loaned by Miss Betty Edden of Thame

Other Edden items on display in the Museum are a set of buttons thought to be from the victim's coat, and a possible murder weapon.

And lastly, this photograph of St Mary's church choir, 1911/2, includes several people who might themselves be termed Amenities, or Human Resources. They are, from back, left to right: A Clarke, W Betts, R Arnott, A Humpris, Mr Green (Postmaster), - Howlett, Mr Smedley (Surveyor), the Relieving Officer, Mr Gurnet (landlord, Cross Keys) C Simmonds, Curate, - - , H Mitchell, - - , F Cornish, F Simmons, H Howes, J Brown (Landlord, the Greyhound) W Howes, J Howes, B Allnutt, F Mitchell, W Cox, C Lane, HJ Webb (Headmaster), - Judge, W Hayes, F Young,- Hobbs, R Lane, H Allnutt.